Be Together

HOW WOMEN *and* MEN
CAN HEAL *the* DIVIDE AND
WORK TOGETHER
TO TRANSFORM *the* FUTURE

STUDY GUIDE | SIX SESSIONS

Danielle Strickland

THOMAS NELSON

Better Together Study Guide

© 2020 by Danielle Strickland

Published in Nashville, Tennessee, by Nelson Books. Nelson Books is a registered trademark of HarperCollins Christian Publishing, Inc.

Published in association with The Bindery Agency, www.The.Bindery.Agency.com.

All Scripture quotations are taken from the Holy Bible, New International Version®. NIV®. Copyright 1973, 1978, 1994, 2011 by Biblica, Inc.®. Used by permission. All rights reserved worldwide.

Thomas Nelson titles may be purchased in bulk for educational, business, fundraising, or sales promotional use. For information, please e-mail SpecialMarkets@ThomasNelson.com.

ISBN 978-0-310-11076-7 (softcover)
ISBN 978-0-310-11077-4 (ebook)

First Printing January 2020 / Printed in the United States of America

Contents

Introduction

How This Study Guide Works

Welcome to the *Better Together Study Guide*, a six-week group experience intended to amplify your growth as you watch the video teachings and read my book *Better Together*. This study guide contains six guided Group Gatherings and six weeks' worth of guided Personal Time of reflection and prayer. My hope is that this experience will help you to digest and embrace the truths you find in *Better Together* by helping you to engage with God and others. Before you dive in, let's take a closer look at what this guide has to offer.

GROUP GATHERINGS

During your guided Group Gatherings you and others will be exploring and discussing what it means to be *Better Together*. Each gathering is designed to be 70–90 minutes and is divided into three main sections: Warm Up, Watch Video, Unpack Together.

WARM UP (5-10 MINUTES)

This is an opportunity for each of you to check in with God and your group before diving into your video session. Though it is the shortest of the three sections, it can have a huge impact on the openness of your group.

WATCH VIDEO (20-22 MINUTES)

Every Group Gathering is set up with a video that explores a specific aspect of being *Better Together*. During the video, you are encouraged to take notes as to what stands out to you and what questions you still have. Each video is roughly 20 minutes and is followed by an opportunity to quickly jot down what resonated with you most and what was most challenging.

UNPACK TOGETHER (35-45 MINUTES)

Most of your Group Gathering will be spent unpacking each session's concept together. Each gathering you will (1) *Discuss Together* the video you just watched and the topic it brought up, (2) *Explore Together* a passage of Scripture and what it means for you today, (3) *Experience Together* a group activity that will help you to engage with that session's topic, and (4) *Pray Together* to close out your meeting.

PERSONAL TIME

In between each gathering there are three days' worth of personal time provided for you to reflect and pray on what you have been learning and experiencing so far. These times with God are not intended to be stress-inducing or burdensome. Rather, they are offered as opportunities for you to process with God what is going on in your heart and mind. You are encouraged to engage in all, some, or any of the activities you find there, while keeping in mind that the more you engage with God in this process, the more your heart will be opened to the transformation that he wants to bring within you.

Okay! You should be all ready to jump in! My prayer is that your eyes, mind, and heart would be opened to what God has for you and your group and that the seeds that are planted here will lead to the shared thriving of women and men for the sake of a better future for us all. Thanks for joining me.

Danielle

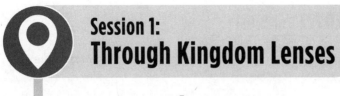

Session 1:
Through Kingdom Lenses

Group Gathering

WARM UP (5–10 minutes)

INVITE GOD IN

Take a few minutes to talk with God silently about the lenses through which you see the world. Ask God where he wants you to pay attention to your worldview.

If it is helpful, use the space below to write, draw, or express yourself to God.

_____

_____

_____

_____

_____

_____

_____

_____

DISCUSS TOGETHER

How do differences normally divide us in our culture? On a daily basis, where and in what ways do you see or experience differences driving us?

WATCH VIDEO (22 minutes)

Watch the video for Group Gathering 1. Feel free to take notes in the space provided.

VIDEO NOTES

_____

_____

_____

_____

_____

John 9:1–12

_____

_____

_____

_____

Finding Fault vs. Taking Responsibility

> "We choose to find fault with current situations when we want to escape responsibility to change them."

_____

_____

_____

_____

_____

Jesus Uses Natural Means

"Jesus uses every natural means necessary. What I mean by this is that Jesus does well. We don't see it coming."

_____

_____

_____

_____

Jesus Uses Supernatural Power

"Jesus infuses natural things with supernatural power."

_____

_____

_____

_____

Jesus Gives People Choices

"Jesus gives people choices."

_____

_____

_____

_____

Galatians 3:26–29

Power Is A Corrupting Influence If . . .

TAKE A MOMENT

Take two minutes to jot down what stood out to you the most about what Danielle said. What resonated with you and what was challenging?

UNPACK TOGETHER (35–45 minutes)

DISCUSS TOGETHER

1. Danielle said that an honest assessment of the lenses we wear is the starting place of shifting our perspective. What makes identifying the flaws of the lenses we wear so important? How can someone safely identify their flawed perspective in a way that is helpful and not shameful?

2. What are some natural means that can be implemented around us to shift the lenses through which we see the world? What would it look like to invite Jesus' supernatural power into those means? How can Christlike empowerment also play a role?

Shifting Martha's Lenses:

Select a volunteer to read aloud to the group:

As Jesus and his disciples were on their way, he came to a village where a woman named Martha opened her home to him. She had a sister called Mary, who sat at the Lord's feet listening to what he said. But Martha was distracted by all the preparations that had to be made. She came to him and asked, "Lord, don't you care that my sister has left me to do the work by myself? Tell her to help me!" "Martha, Martha," the Lord answered, "you are worried and upset about many things, but few things are needed—or indeed only one. Mary has chosen what is better, and it will not be taken away from her."
(Luke 10:38–42)

EXPLORE TOGETHER

Group leader: select a volunteer to read the following passage and commentary aloud. Discuss the questions below.

So in Christ Jesus you are all children of God through faith, for all of you who were baptized into Christ have clothed yourselves with Christ. There is neither Jew nor Gentile, neither slave nor free, nor is there male and female, for you are all one in Christ Jesus. If you belong to Christ, then you are Abraham's seed, and heirs according to the promise.
(Galatians 3:26–29)

Gentile was a term describing any person of non-Jewish descent. In the New Testament non-Jewish persons are also referred to as Greek, given the heavy Greco-Roman influence throughout the Ancient Near East.

What It Meant Then:

As Paul writes this passionate yet heart-broken letter to the churches of Galatia, some major worldview shifts were under way for early Christians. Jesus' life-giving and radically inclusive message was spreading quickly across the known world, and not just among the Jewish community. The Holy Spirit was drawing both Jew and Gentile alike to receive new life in Christ. Though beautiful in so many ways, the coming together of various cultures, backgrounds, and worldviews led to a lot of conflict among early Christians.

In the church in Galatia, a small group of Jewish Christians were pressuring Gentile believers to adhere to Jewish religious and cultural practices, claiming that salvation is perfected through them. These practices and beliefs were deeply ingrained into the Jewish way of life. This group even encouraged other Jewish Christians not to associate with Gentile believers who refused to bend to their pressure. Paul, a Jewish Christian himself, took huge exception to this, pointing out that all believers' salvation and growth happen through the power of Christ alone (Galatians 3:1–3). He claimed that the Jewish customs were no longer necessary and that there was no hope for salvation through Jewish religious law (Galatians 3:10–14).

In the passage on page 11, Paul challenges the worldview of both Jews and Gentiles, putting to rest the notion that there should be divisions among believers based on differences. Society of that time was stratified based on race, status, and gender. Those with the right qualifications would be elevated to certain levels of cultural and societal privilege while others were discriminated against. By using three consecutive pairs of opposites (Jew/Gentile, slave/free, male/female), Paul rejects three major dividing lines in first-century culture.

He even goes as far as saying that all who belong to Christ are *Abraham's seed*, a privilege previously bestowed on the Jewish people exclusively. In this Paul was admonishing followers of Jesus to see the world and others through the new kingdom lenses of inclusion, love, and equality.

What It Means Now:

Paul outlines the cultural worldview that Jesus was calling his followers to embrace. Much like in the first century, our culture has a subtle yet powerful impact on the way we see the world and those around us. Recognizing and setting aside the lenses we wear is no small task, yet it is a necessary one if we are ever to see the shared thriving of humanity that Jesus desires. Christ has established new cultural viewpoints and norms for his followers to adhere to—ones where we are all children of God in Christ and on an equal footing regardless of our differences. Paul writes that we are *all one in Christ Jesus*, and it will take us all working together in order to shift these entrenched perspectives.

> Abraham was the first patriarch of the Israelite people to whom God promised to bless extensively. Being *Abraham's Seed* is a way of saying that all those in Christ (including Gentiles) would receive the same rights and privileges that God promised to Abraham's descendants. This would have been a radical claim in Paul's time and likely met with fierce opposition.

Looking Ahead

1. What do you think made it so difficult for Jewish Christians to shift their worldview and see others through Jesus' lenses? What made changing lenses so important for the early church?

2. What similarities and differences do you notice between a first-century approach to diversity and our culture's approach today? How have you seen the church embrace kingdom lenses? How have you seen the church embrace the lenses of our world?

3. Where in your own life have you noticed difficulty putting on Jesus' kingdom lenses of equality and love? What would it look like to start to better embrace that worldview with the support of Jesus and those around you?

EXPERIENCE TOGETHER

Instructions:

- Have one person read the guided prayer on pages 16–17 out loud to the group.

- As they read, take time to think about and pray about a situation in your life where you are struggling to see someone or something through Jesus' kingdom lenses.

- If needed, take notes as you go in the open space provided on the next page. After you are finished with the guided prayer, give everyone a few extra minutes to jot down any final thoughts from the prayer time.

- When everyone is ready, discuss your experience as a group. How does Jesus want to be present in that situation with you? How does he want to shift your perspective?

- Have the group encourage each member as they share.

> As the reader, make sure you are also engaging in prayer for yourself as you read.

PRAY TOGETHER

Have someone close your time in prayer by inviting God into the rest of this week. Ask Jesus to shift your worldview to better align with his.

GUIDED PRAYER

Before you begin, take a few minutes to yourself to think about a situation where you have struggled to love, respect, or include someone. It can be something you are currently experiencing or a situation from your past. Once everyone is ready, have one person read the following aloud as your group engages in this guided prayer. Reader, use the paragraph breaks to pause for at least 30 seconds. After you are done with the guided prayer, give everyone a few extra minutes to jot down any final thoughts from the prayer time.

Imagine you are in a place that is especially peaceful for you. It can be a place in nature, a special place in your home, or somewhere else entirely.

_____

_____

Now imagine Jesus is there with you. He smiles, bringing you even more peace. How is he engaging with you?

_____

_____

Knowing that you are fully loved and accepted, tell him about the situation where you are struggling to love, respect, or include someone.

_____

_____

Open up to Jesus about the situation, letting him know your thoughts and feelings about the situation and person. How does Jesus empathize with your thoughts and feelings?

_____

_____

Now Jesus points out something to you that you notice for the first
time. You are wearing a pair of dirty glasses. Glasses through which
you are seeing this situation. Jesus gives the glasses a name. What is the
name Jesus gives your glasses?

_____

_____

_____

He asks you to notice how the glasses are shaping the way you see this
situation. He offers to clean your glasses in a way only he can. Will you
let him? Imagine handing him your glasses.

_____

_____

_____

After cleaning your glasses, he offers them back to you. As he hands
them to you, he gives them a new name and perspective through which
to see the situation. What new name does he give to them? . . . Notice
how they change your perspective on the situation.

_____

_____

_____

As you both get ready to leave together, thank Jesus for this gift he has
given you.

_____

_____

_____

_____

_____

17

Personal Study

The following pages are for your personal study in between sessions. Engage in any or all of these three times of prayer and reflection in order to enhance your experience.

DAY · 1

"We can change [our lenses] by embracing the truth, imagining the possibilities, and confronting the barriers. We need to trade our patriarchal glasses for some clearer lenses." **Danielle Strickland,** ***Better Together*, Chapter 7**

 READ

The LORD does not look at the things people look at. People look at the outward appearance, but the LORD looks at the heart. **(1 Samuel 16:7b)**

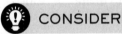 CONSIDER

Where in my life do I *look at things the way people* do? List the areas here:

_____

_____

_____

_____

_____

_____

_____

_____

What would it look like to start seeing things the way the Lord does?

_____

_____

_____

_____

STEP OUT

Take the next 24 hours to really notice the way you are viewing others around you through the lens of external factors and stereotypes. As it comes up, invite God to transform your lens.

PRAY

Make a list of all the ways you are tempted to judge people based on external factors. Ask God how he wants you to see those around you through his eyes.

_____

_____

_____

_____

_____

_____

_____

LOOKING FOR MORE?

Read Chapter 5 of _Better Together_ by Danielle Strickland and write down what stands out to you most.

DAY · 2

"If we are going to adjust our lives to fit the new social constructs of power we have got to do the work of identifying our own. How will we ever change something we are not recognizing or acknowledging? So what kind of power/privilege do we have?" **Danielle Strickland,** *Better Together*, **Chapter 10**

 READ

Do not conform to the pattern of this world, but be transformed by the renewing of your mind. Then you will be able to test and approve what God's will is—his good, pleasing and perfect will. **(Romans 12:2)**

 CONSIDER

In what ways am I conforming to the pattern of this world when it comes to the relationships of women and men? Define the ways here and then take time to write the obvious or potential consequences of conforming.

Where do I need Jesus to transform and renew my mind? What specifically are you asking Jesus to transform, to renew? Be clear and declare your need. Honest vulnerability of need tills the soul's soil for growth.

 **STEP OUT**

Intentionally talk to three people outside your group this week about what you are learning in this group and how it is impacting you. Set a reminder on your phone if necessary.

 PRAY

Spend some time deeply considering with God what areas of your worldview need transformation and alignment with Jesus'. Ask God how you might cooperate with the transformation he wants to do in you.

_____

_____

_____

_____

_____

_____

_____

_____

_____

_____

_____

_____

_____

LOOKING FOR MORE?

Read all of Romans 12. What do you learn about the new culture Jesus wants to build for the church and ultimately the world?

DAY · 3

"When things get personal, they get closer and our perspective shifts. Far from talking about the 'theory' of empowerment, the conversation moves towards a felt need to change for the sake of our daughters and sons. It's an important shift." **Danielle Strickland,** *Better Together***, Chapter 7**

 READ

Dear friends, do not believe every spirit, but test the spirits to see whether they are from God, because many false prophets have gone out into the world. **(1 John 4:1)**

Discerning spirits is a way of staying in tune with the Holy Spirit, understanding when a prophet or teaching comes from God and when one does not.

 CONSIDER

How am I allowing beliefs or understandings not from God to guide my life (particularly in the area of inequality)? Describe here.

_____

_____

_____

_____

_____

_____

Describe would it look like to tune myself with the Holy Spirit and his worldview.

_____

_____

_____

_____

_____

STEP OUT

Ask a trusted friend if you can talk together about the lenses of inequality you both want to release. Discuss ways Jesus might see differently and pray for one another.

PRAY

Spend some time asking and listening to God about what lie/s you are believing in the area of gender equality. After rejecting each lie in Jesus' name, ask him what truth he wants to replace the lie with.

_____

_____

_____

_____

_____

LOOKING FOR MORE?

Read Chapter 6 of _Better Together_ by Danielle Strickland and write down what stands out to you most.

Notes

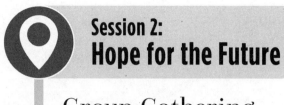

Hope for the Future

Group Gathering

WARM UP (5–10 minutes)

INVITE GOD IN

Take a few minutes to talk with God silently about how you are personally feeling about doing this study. Where are you excited? Where are you apprehensive? Open your heart to him and invite him to transform you where he may.

If it is helpful, use the space below to write, draw, or express yourself to God.

_____

_____

_____

_____

_____

_____

_____

_____

DISCUSS TOGETHER

How would you define hope? What do you think makes hope so powerful?

WATCH VIDEO (21 minutes)

Watch the video for Group Gathering 2. Feel free to take notes in the space provided.

VIDEO NOTES

_____

_____

_____

_____

It is time for women and men to start thriving together.

"It's about the conviction that it's time for women and men to start thriving together, to create a better future for our sons and our daughters."

_____

_____

_____

The seemingly impossible is actually possible now.

"Sometimes things that seem impossible or at least a way distant possibility are actually possible and possible right now."

_____

_____

_____

_____

Imagine your best future.

"When you imagine your best future, the one you want to see your kids live, what do you see?"

Imagine a better world and understand oppression.

"She told me two things were necessary. The first was we had to imagine a better world. The second thing required to change nations? Understand oppression."

Bring beauty the intersection of despair.

"You could join the amazing folks trying to change this world, trying to bring beauty right into the intersection of despair."

TAKE A MOMENT

Take two minutes to jot down what stood out to you the most about what Danielle said. What resonated with you and what was challenging?

_____

_____

_____

_____

_____

UNPACK TOGETHER (35–45 minutes)

DISCUSS TOGETHER

1. Danielle said it's time for women and men to start thriving together. What does the shared thriving of women and men look like to you? When considering this shared thriving, how do you imagine the best future for you and/or your kids?

2. What do you think starting with our destination in mind means? Discuss what your group's better future looks like and how you can dream together for transformation.

EXPLORE TOGETHER

Group leader, read the following passage and commentary aloud. Discuss the questions below.

This is what the LORD says: "When seventy years are completed for Babylon, I will come to you and fulfill my good promise to bring you back to this place. For I know the plans I have for you," declares the LORD, "plans to prosper you and not to harm you, plans to give you hope and a future. Then you will call on me and come and pray to me, and I will listen to you. You will seek me and find me when you seek me with all your heart." **(Jeremiah 29:10–13)**

What It Meant Then:

This often-quoted verse giving hope to so many comes right in the middle of one of the most difficult times in Israel's history. The divided nation of Israel had already seen the Northern Kingdom overrun by the Assyrian Empire, and it was only a matter of time before the Southern Kingdom of Judah would face a similar fate. Jeremiah warned Judah that if they would not turn away from their evil way of living and idolatry, God would allow the rising Babylonian Empire to overtake them. Judah's refusal to return to the Lord led to their eventual downfall, with the destruction of Jerusalem and the temple and the exile of large portions of the population at the hands of the Babylonian king, Nebuchadnezzar.

Giving the Hopeless Hope:

Select a volunteer to read aloud to the group:

And a woman was there who had been subject to bleeding for twelve years, but no one could heal her. She came up behind him and touched the edge of his cloak, and immediately her bleeding stopped. "Who touched me?" Jesus asked. When they all denied it, Peter said, "Master, the people are crowding and pressing against you."

But Jesus said, "Someone touched me; I know that power has gone out from me." Then the woman, seeing that she could not go unnoticed, came trembling and fell at his feet. In the presence of all the people, she told why she had touched him and how she had been instantly healed. Then he said to her, "Daughter, your faith has healed you. Go in peace." **(Luke 8:43–48)**

Despite Israel's unfaithfulness, God offered hope to his people in captivity. The passage above kicks off a section of prophetic promise for the Israelites' future. Through Jeremiah,

29

the Lord vowed to one day rescue his people and bring them back to their land. God goes on in this hope-filled section to promise a new covenant with his people and points forward to the coming of a Messiah, revealed hundreds of years later to be Jesus of Nazareth (Jeremiah 31:31; 33:15; also see Hebrews 8:8). The exiled nation clung to these promises of hope, and God used them as a North Star to guide his people back to him.

What It Means Now:

Though the promise above concerns a specific event in Israel's history, the full extent of that promise only truly comes in and through Jesus and, as a result, can extend to us today. God still frequently uses hopeful visions of the future to keep us going in times of difficulty and draw us toward repentance and transformation. What's more, in Christ we get to be a part of God's redemptive work here on earth (Matthew 5:13–16), bringing his deliverance from injustice and oppression through the body of Christ (1 Corinthians 12). Thus Jeremiah 29 can serve as a hopeful reminder of what is to come and an ever-present beacon leading us toward a fuller realization of God's kingdom here on earth.

1. How do you think the promise from God in the passage above helped the Israelites come back to God during their exile? How can the impact of hope in God transform the future of a person or people?

2. What is the personal and cultural impact of knowing that God's promise in the passage above extends to you through Christ? Describe real-life examples where you see humanity work with and against God's *plans to prosper* us.

3. Where in your world do you see a need for God's promise of hope (particularly considering the inequality between women and men)? How do you want to work with God in his plan to prosper those around you with shared thriving?

EXPERIENCE TOGETHER

Supplies:

- 5 sticky notes per person

- Pens

Instructions:

- On the sticky notes, take a few minutes to have all members of the group write down five hopeful visions of the future when it comes to the thriving of women and men together. Each vision should be contained in a word or phrase.

- Once everyone is finished, place the notes for the entire group in a cluster on the wall.

- Take turns having each member of the group pick a word or phrase they did not write themselves that stands out to them. Have them explain what that particular vision stirs in them.

- Once everyone has shared, briefly discuss how the hope-filled experience has impacted you.

PRAY TOGETHER

Have someone close your time in prayer by inviting God into the rest of this week. Ask that his good plan would be worked in and through the members of the group.

Personal Study

The following pages are for your personal study in between sessions. Consider engaging in any or all of these three times of prayer and reflection in order to enhance your experience.

DAY · 1

> "This is why we call it good news. It's a restoration agenda that seeks to move everyone towards transformation. Including the relationships between women and men." **Danielle Strickland, *Better Together*, Chapter 1**

 READ

So God created mankind in his own image, in the image of God he created them; male and female he created them. **(Genesis 1:27)**

 CONSIDER

What do I think makes men and women better together?

_____

_____

_____

Describe how both male and female together represent a fuller image of God.

_____

_____

_____

In what circumstances, situations, relationships is the image of God most apparent and least apparent? Why do you think that is?

_____

_____

_____

🎯 STEP OUT

Over the next day, make a point to pay attention to the interactions you see between women and men around you (including your own). As you do, ask God how his will is being done and how it is not in those interactions.

🙏 PRAY

Talk with God about your feelings toward the inequality women experience in our world. Don't be afraid to be honest with God about what you feel (sadness, anger, helplessness, apathy). Ask him how he wants to better align your heart and will with his.

_____

_____

_____

_____

👓 LOOKING FOR MORE?

Read Chapter 1 of _Better Together_ by Danielle Strickland and write down what stands out to you most.

_____

_____

33

DAY · 2

"Realizing true equality will require the empowerment of women. And empowering women will have an incredible impact on shaping a better future." **Danielle Strickland, *Better Together*, Chapter 2**

 READ

Not only so, but we also glory in our sufferings, because we know that suffering produces perseverance; perseverance, character; and character, hope. And hope does not put us to shame, because God's love has been poured out into our hearts through the Holy Spirit, who has been given to us. **(Romans 5:3–5)**

 CONSIDER

Take honest stock of your daily life. How are women around me suffering in the face of gender inequality?

_____

_____

_____

_____

What might I do to represent God's hope to them? List a few other examples and commit to follow through.

_____

_____

_____

_____

 **STEP OUT**

Text one woman an encouragement letting her know how you see God empowering her and using her to accomplish his good purposes.

 PRAY

Ask God how he would like to see the world around you change for the better when it comes to the shared thriving of both women and men. Spend some time just listening to him.

_____

_____

_____

_____

_____

_____

_____

_____

LOOKING FOR MORE?

Read all of Romans 5. What does it reveal about hope in the face of difficulty?

_____

_____

_____

_____

DAY · 3

"And I remain completely convinced through the Scriptures that true mutuality is the original sacred design of humanity. Men and women are meant to work together for the flourishing of the world."
Danielle Strickland, *Better Together*, Chapter 1

 READ

May the God of hope fill you with all joy and peace as you trust in him, so that you may overflow with hope by the power of the Holy Spirit. **(Romans 15:13)**

CONSIDER

How and in what ways do I need my God of hope today?

_____

_____

_____

_____

_____

Where does my community need his hope when it comes to gender inequality?

_____

_____

_____

_____

_____

_____

 STEP OUT

Set aside time in the next week to partner with the opposite gender in doing something positive. Pick someone you feel comfortable with, like a friend or family member. It can be as small as planting a plant together or as big as planning a fundraiser to help liberate women from sex slavery. Be creative and don't be afraid to be intentional.

 PRAY

Ask God how the shared thriving of both women and men can help the world to flourish. Write down what comes to your mind and heart. Tell him how you want to be a part of that shared thriving.

_____

_____

_____

_____

_____

_____

_____

_____

 LOOKING FOR MORE?

Read Chapter 2 of *Better Together* by Danielle Strickland and write down what stands out to you most.

_____

_____

_____

_____

Notes

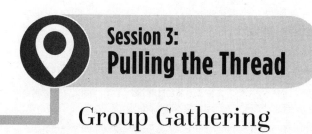

Pulling the Thread

Group Gathering

WARM UP (5–10 minutes)

INVITE GOD IN

Take a few minutes to review your week with Jesus. What did you experience? What did you do? What did you feel? What personal connections stood out? Simply tell Jesus as you would a friend and allow him to highlight what he wants you to notice.

If it is helpful, use the space below to write, draw, or express yourself to God.

_____

_____

_____

_____

_____

_____

_____

DISCUSS TOGETHER

What stood out to you the most about your past week's Personal Study time? How did you see God instill in you hope for the future, and what still felt hopeless? Where in your week did you see the shared thriving of women and men (or lack thereof)?

WATCH VIDEO (20 minutes)

Watch the video for Group Gathering 3. Feel free to take notes in the space provided.

VIDEO NOTES

_____

_____

_____

_____

_____

Oppression is like a current.

> "Oppression is like a current in our culture . . . a cultural current that leads us to dangerous places."

_____

_____

_____

_____

_____

1 John 3:8 – Destroying the Devil's Work

_____

_____

_____

_____

_____

John 10:10 – The Thief

_____

_____

_____

_____

_____

Oppression happens to us *and* in us.

> "Jesus understands that oppression is not just something that happens to us. It's something that also happens in us. And he wants to partner with us in the loosening of that inner oppression."

_____

_____

_____

_____

_____

Pay attention to your loose ends.

> "Pay attention to the loose end in your life. Don't dismiss it. Don't pretend like it doesn't exist. It's a loose end and can be the beginning of an unraveling that's necessary to undo the oppression that is at work in us."

_____

_____

_____

_____

Participating in redemption will take some effort.

"Jesus is inviting us to participate in the great redemption plan toward reconciliation, but here's an important thing to know. It will take some effort."

_____

_____

_____

_____

_____

Joy is a lubricant of change.

"Joy, I've found, is a lubricant of change. It moves us forward together. It helps us to acknowledge where we've come and that we can do even more."

_____

_____

_____

_____

_____

TAKE A MOMENT

Danielle said the first step to unraveling oppression is to identify the loose end in your own life (the area or belief that is working with our culture of oppression rather than against it). Take two minutes to talk with God silently about what your loose ends may be and how he wants you to start to pull on them. Notice your areas of resistance and ask God what is behind them.

_____

_____

_____

_____

UNPACK TOGETHER (35–45 minutes)

DISCUSS TOGETHER

1. What do you think Danielle means when saying our culture has *a current of oppression*? What are some helpful ways to guard against simply going with the flow of that current?

2. What could it look like for someone to invite Jesus into their personal unraveling? How can you work with Jesus to bring about this process?

Jesus Declares His Mission:

Select a volunteer to read aloud to the group:

He went to Nazareth, where he had been brought up, and on the Sabbath day he went into the synagogue, as was his custom. He stood up to read, and the scroll of the prophet Isaiah was handed to him. Unrolling it, he found the place where it is written: "The Spirit of the Lord is on me, because he has anointed me to proclaim good news to the poor. He has sent me to proclaim freedom for the prisoners and recovery of sight for the blind, to set the oppressed free, to proclaim the year of the Lord's favor." **(Luke 4:16–19)**

EXPLORE TOGETHER

Group leader, read the following passage and commentary aloud. Discuss the questions below.

Therefore Jesus said again, "Very truly I tell you, I am the gate for the sheep. All who have come before me are thieves and robbers, but the sheep have not listened to them. I am the gate; whoever enters through me will be saved. They will come in and go out, and find pasture. The thief comes only to steal and kill and destroy; I have come that they may have life, and have it to the full." **(John 10:7–10)**

What It Meant Then:

In the passage above, Jesus is halfway through an address to a group of Pharisees that had just thrown a man out of their presence to whom Jesus had given sight (John 9:34). Jesus suggests that the Pharisees themselves are spiritually blind (John 9:39) and uses a picture of sheep, shepherds, and thieves to illustrate what they are like.

The Pharisees, though well-known antagonists in the Gospel stories, at the time were highly respected spiritual leaders of the Jewish people. They represented a system of oppression that was well accepted and complexly woven into the fabric of that society. Their stringent and judgmental religious system ostracized many (especially the poor, the sick, outsiders, and those considered unclean) and made the life God had to offer seemingly unattainable. This is why Jesus paints them to be *thieves* and *robbers* (v. 8) coming to *steal*, *kill*, and *destroy* (v. 10) the sheep (God's people). All they had to offer was a way that led to death and destruction.

Jesus, on the other hand, is *the gate* (v. 7) through which the sheep will find both the protection of the pen and the life of the pasture. He says *whoever enters through him will be saved*, and he has come so that they may *have life to the full*. In this, Jesus offers a way of life opposed

44

to the Pharisees' oppression. To those who follow Jesus, it is clear that this abundant life is available now (and is not just a promise for the afterlife). Jesus uses this opportunity in John 10 to stand against the evil and death that came through this oppressive system by instead demonstrating himself to be the God who pursues the lost and freely offers *life to the full* (v. 10).

What It Means Now:

The dynamic between the Good Shepherd, who offers us a full life, and that which comes to steal, kill, and destroy is still very much at play. Just as Jesus' abundant life is available to us today through the Holy Spirit (John 6:63), oppressive and evil systems like that of the Pharisees also still exist. Though Jesus ultimately will bring about the restoration of all things (Acts 3:21), he desires that we, filled with his Spirit, work as his body, continuing his ministry here on earth (1 Corinthians 12). It is also clear that Jesus calls his people to stand against oppression of all kinds and stand instead for love. (See Zechariah 7:10; Matthew 25:31–46; Ephesians 6:11.) Thus we join Jesus in his restoration work to end oppression through loving others and pointing them to Christ, the source of true life.

1. What do you think Jesus meant when he said that *thieves come to steal, kill, and destroy*? Given this criteria, who or what are the modern-day *thieves* in our world?

2. What would it look like for someone to lean into the *life to the full* that Jesus has to offer? How can learning to listen for Jesus, our Good Shepherd, help us stand against oppression in our world?

3. How might God be calling you to oppose the systems of oppression around you (especially when it comes to gender inequality)? How can you instead practically point others to the abundant life Jesus has to offer?

EXPERIENCE TOGETHER

Supplies:

- Whiteboard or large sticky-note easel pad

- Marker

Instructions:

- Choose a scribe to write down notes on the whiteboard or large sticky-note easel pad.

- All together, brainstorm ways that you as a group can help to unravel systems of oppression (particularly around gender inequality) in your group, community, or organization. Make sure they are not just ideas of equality, but practical steps that can actually change the way things are working.

Some ideas might include:

creating regular opportunities for the shared leadership of both women and men, putting into action corrective experiences that challenge harmful stereotypes, coming up with creative ways to join Jesus in destroying the oppressive works of the devil in your city or town, etc.

- After brainstorming, choose three practical goals that can act as markers for your group to track your momentum as you journey together. Think of things that are powerful enough to actually make a difference in your group but practical enough that they can be implemented in the next four weeks.

- Also spend time planning and writing down the *How* (how you intend to achieve these goals) and the *When* (when you plan on implementing this action step) for each of your three goals. Use the worksheets on the next pages to record your group goals.

- At the beginning of future sessions, check in on how you are doing as a group with implementing the action steps and accomplishing your goals. Celebrate the goals you implement and encourage each other in the ones you have yet to accomplish.

PRAY TOGETHER

Have someone close your time in prayer by inviting God into the rest of this week. Ask that he would make this group aware of their loose threads and give them the courage to start to pull.

GROUP GOALS

▶ GOAL 1:

_____

_____

_____

_____

The How:

_____

_____

_____

_____

_____

The When:

_____

_____

_____

_____

_____

▶ GOAL 2:

_____

_____

_____

_____

The How:

_____
_____
_____
_____

The When:

_____
_____
_____
_____

▶ GOAL 3:

_____
_____
_____
_____

The How:

_____
_____
_____
_____

The When:

_____
_____
_____
_____

Personal Study

The following pages are for your personal study in between sessions. Engage in any or all of these three times of prayer and reflection in order to enhance your experience.

DAY · 1

> "The church without the centrality of the cross is just a community group. But the cross, that is where true power is on display for the deepest wounds of the world." **Danielle Strickland, *Better Together*, Chapter 4**

 READ

May the Lord make your love increase and overflow for each other and for everyone else, just as ours does for you. May he strengthen your hearts so that you will be blameless and holy in the presence of our God and Father when our Lord Jesus comes with all his holy ones. **(1 Thessalonians 3:12–13)**

 CONSIDER

Where do I need the Lord to *strengthen my heart* and *make my love for others increase*? What internal oppression does Jesus what to unravel in me? Be honest with yourself, and describe what you need to unravel here:

_____

_____

_____

_____

 STEP OUT

Danielle said that noticing the *loose ends* in our own lives is the beginning of unraveling the oppression that is at work in us personally. Spend some time thinking through and writing down the loose ends you notice in your own life and heart.

> *Loose Ends* are areas or beliefs in us that are working with a culture of oppression rather than against it.

_____

_____

_____

Consider tying some yarn around your wrist or key chain this week to remind you to keep an eye out for these personal loose ends.

 PRAY

Knowing that you are fully forgiven in Christ, spend some time confessing your loose ends to God. Ask him how he wants to transform your heart so that those areas begin to unravel.

_____

_____

_____

 LOOKING FOR MORE?

Read Chapter 3 of *Better Together* by Danielle Strickland and write down what stands out to you most.

DAY · 2

"Like a bacteria, sexism has entered our collective body and we are dying from the infection. The time for a proper diagnosis has come."
Danielle Strickland, *Better Together*, Chapter 3

 READ

You, my brothers and sisters, were called to be free. But do not use your freedom to indulge the flesh; rather, serve one another humbly in love. For the entire law is fulfilled in keeping this one command: "Love your neighbor as yourself." **(Galatians 5:13–14)**

 CONSIDER

How am I using my freedom to *indulge in the flesh*?

_____

_____

_____

"The flesh" is a term biblical authors use to describe the sinful nature and habituations that are common among all humanity.

Define how loving my neighbor as myself will contribute to the shared thriving of both women and men in my community and immediate area of influence.

_____

_____

_____

_____

 **STEP OUT**

Using the format of the *Group Goals Worksheet* on page 48, create three of your own personal goals, explaining how you want to start pulling on the loose ends in your life. Think of things that are powerful enough to actually make a difference in your life, yet practical enough that they can be implemented in the next four weeks. Also record the *How* (how you intend to achieve the goal) and the *When* (when you plan on implementing the action steps) for each of your three goals.

 PRAY

Talk to God about your three goals and invite him into the unraveling process. Spend some time asking him for his wisdom, guidance, and strength.

_____

_____

_____

_____

_____

_____

_____

LOOKING FOR MORE?

Read all of Galatians 5. Record how *walking in step with the Spirit* is vital in unraveling the current of oppression around you.

DAY · 3

"It's a transformational idea to suggest that our restored relationship with God would begin to restore our relationships with everything and everyone else. Indeed it's the gospel. A good description of the gospel itself is the 'ministry of reconciliation.'" **Danielle Strickland, Better Together, Chapter 4**

 READ

He has shown you, O mortal, what is good. And what does the Lord require of you? To act justly and to love mercy and to walk humbly with your God. **(Micah 6:8)**

 CONSIDER

Where might I be going along with the current of *injustice* and *unmercifulness* in our culture?

Write down a few areas or circumstances you are aware of right now.

How can *walking humbly with my God* help me start to unravel this oppression around me? What will this look like, practically?

_____

_____

_____

_____

_____

 STEP OUT

Spend some time thinking of someone making strides to bring gender equity in the world around them. Find a small way to celebrate with them what they are doing. You could send them a note, take them out to lunch, or affirm them publicly. Be sure to consider what they would be most comfortable with and what they would experience as honoring.

 PRAY

Spend some time praying through each of the following phrases from Micah 6:8 and what God might be calling you to in each of them. Ask him how you can bring about an unraveling of gender inequality through them.

- *Act Justly*

- *Love Mercy*

- *Walk Humbly with Your God*

_____

_____

_____

_____

_____

_____

_____

_____

_____

LOOKING FOR MORE?

Read Chapter 4 of *Better Together* by Danielle Strickland and write down what stands out to you most.

Notes

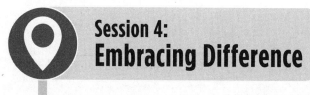

Session 4:
Embracing Difference

Group Gathering

WARM UP (5–10 minutes)

INVITE GOD IN

Take a few minutes to talk with God silently about your experience in this group so far. What has shifted your perspective the most? What is still challenging you? Just be honest with God about where you are right now.

If it is helpful, use the space below to write, draw, or express yourself to God.

_____

_____

_____

_____

_____

_____

_____

_____

DISCUSS TOGETHER

Briefly check in on how the Group Goals you decided on last session have progressed. Take a few minutes to talk through how you can continue to take steps forward as a group.

WATCH VIDEO (22 minutes)

Watch the video for Group Gathering 4. Feel free to take notes in the space provided.

VIDEO NOTES

_____

_____

_____

_____

The cross is the center of all transformation.

> "I started to understand on a deep level that the cross is at the center of all transformation."

_____

_____

_____

_____

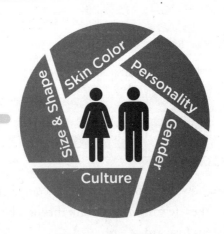

Equity: the opportunity to use the rights one has been given

"Equality is about our rights, but equity is about our opportunity to use them."

_____

_____

_____

_____

Exodus 1:1–10 – Pharaoh's fear of the Israelites

_____

_____

_____

_____

Difference is nothing to fear. It is something to celebrate.

"Difference is nothing to fear."

DIFFERENCE

MUTUALITY

Mutuality: the idea that we are all connected to each other in meaningful ways

"Mutuality is the idea that we're all connected to each other in a meaningful way."

_____

_____

_____

_____

Proximity: closeness for the sake of knowing each other as human beings

"Proximity. Let's get to know each other, not as men and women, but as human beings filled with wonder and gifts and potential, expose our past prejudices, and take risks to celebrate who we were always made to be."

_____

_____

_____

_____

TAKE A MOMENT

Take two minutes to jot down what stood out to you the most about what Danielle said. What resonated with you and what was challenging?

_____

_____

_____

_____

UNPACK TOGETHER (35–45 minutes)

DISCUSS TOGETHER

1. What do you think Danielle means when saying the cross is where those who want a new future can meet and start building together? How is Jesus' work on the cross indispensable when it comes to women and men healing and moving forward together?

2. When building a transformed future for women and men brick by brick, how is equity an important building block? How is mutuality?

Love Beyond Difference:

Select a volunteer to read aloud to the group:

Now he had to go through Samaria. So he came to a town in Samaria called Sychar, near the plot of ground Jacob had given to his son Joseph. Jacob's well was there, and Jesus, tired as he was from the journey, sat down by the well. It was about noon. When a Samaritan woman came to draw water, Jesus said to her, "Will you give me a drink?" (His disciples had gone into the town to buy food.) The Samaritan woman said to him, "You are a Jew and I am a Samaritan woman. How can you ask me for a drink?" (For Jews do not associate with Samaritans.) Jesus answered her, "If you knew the gift of God and who it is that asks you for a drink, you would have asked him and he would have given you living water." **(John 4:4–10)**

EXPLORE TOGETHER

Group leader, read the following passage and commentary aloud. Discuss the questions below.

Just as a body, though one, has many parts, but all its many parts form one body, so it is with Christ . . . The eye cannot say to the hand, "I don't need you!" And the head cannot say to the feet, "I don't need you!" On the contrary, those parts of the body that seem to be weaker are indispensable, and the parts that we think are less honorable we treat with special honor. And the parts that are unpresentable are treated with special modesty, while our presentable parts need no special treatment. But God has put the body together, giving greater honor to the parts that lacked it, so that there should be no division in the body, but that its parts should have equal concern for each other. **(1 Corinthians 12:12, 21–25)**

Corinth was a major port city and economic center in first-century Greece. According to Acts 18, Paul had strategically planted a church there made up of both Jews and Gentiles. After spending much time in the city, he moved on with his missionary journey but would correspond often with the church.

What It Meant Then:

In his first letter to the church in Corinth, Paul used the human body as an illustrative parallel for the church community as a whole. The church body in Corinth had many problems that Paul addressed in his letter. The community had split into a number of divisions, and infighting had become rampant. Furthermore, there were some who sought to elevate those with specific gifts above those with others. All of this tension led Paul into this teaching on the church and how they might embrace unity despite their diversity.

The human body becomes a helpful picture for Paul's teaching, as it is made up of incredibly diverse parts all working together for a common goal. Furthermore, if the body was made up of only one part, it would cease to be able to function (1 Corinthians 12:17). Paul's point is that it is exactly because of the body's diversity that it is an effective and powerful force. Superiority or self-sufficiency hinders it greatly. Not only is the church a body, but Paul goes as far as saying that all believers make up the "body of Christ" (1 Corinthians 12:27). This means that the whole church, empowered by the Holy Spirit, is to work together for the sake of continuing the will and ministry of Jesus on earth.

> Though Paul is referencing diversity in gifting, service, and types of works, it is clear that diverse perspectives, cultures, and races played a role in the division of the Corinthian church. Paul's teaching undoubtedly calls for unity in response to all kinds of diversity.

What It Means Now:

Paul's teaching is still incredibly relevant for the church today. The global church is as diverse as it has ever been, and functioning with unity and harmony is more challenging than ever. Given the differences in race, culture, tradition, language, background, socioeconomic status, theology, and the like, divisions in the body of Christ are at an all-time high. And that does not even include gender differences.

Though messy, unity in the midst of diversity is paramount for the collective community of Christ followers. Jesus calls his church to be marked by love, equality, and the celebration of diversity, noting the strengthening impact of welcoming such differences. The culture where our differences denigrate, elevate, or separate us is to be pushed aside, in favor of allowing the Holy Spirit to unify us in continuing the work of Christ.

Furthermore, Paul makes an argument for equity in the church, encouraging the community to take special consideration of those some might think less honorable or unpresentable. He calls for them to be elevated in special ways. As we look at the current church landscape, it may help us to consider who is treated less honorably and what it would look like to give special honor to them. Though we are all different, each member of Christ's body plays an important role in Jesus' work here on earth. That is why just a verse later, Paul writes, "If one part suffers, every part suffers with it; if one part is honored, every part rejoices with it" (1 Corinthians 12:26). In Christ we are all one and on equal footing in his body. We are all uniquely gifted children of God.

1. How is Paul's illustration of a body with its many parts helpful when thinking about diversity in the church? How have you seen differences be used to strengthen a group?

2. How do you see our world responding to differences and diversity? How can superiority and self-sufficiency in the face of our differences hinder the church and Jesus' mission?

3. Where would you like to embrace difference more? How can you use the concept of equity to bring honor and opportunity to those who need it?

EXPERIENCE TOGETHER

Supplies:

- One sheet of paper per person

- One pen per person·

- Phone or kitchen timer

Instructions:

- Write each member of your group's name on a sheet of paper or cardstock. Tape each paper to the wall around the room.

- Set a timer for 10 minutes and have everyone move around the room, writing an affirmation on each sheet highlighting a unique strength they have seen in that person.

● When you are finished, come back together and take turns having another member of the group read those strengths over each person. Discuss how these strengths make your group better together.

PRAY TOGETHER

Have someone close your time in prayer by inviting God into the rest of this week. Ask that his good plan would be worked in and through the members of the group.

Personal Study

The following pages are for your personal study in between sessions. Engage in any or all of these three times of prayer and reflection in order to enhance your experience.

DAY · 1

"It is a completely natural impulse to want to put distance between yourself and the things you are afraid of. . . . But the stark reality is that this approach fuels the problem. How will we ever rid the room of its spider when we simply shut the door and carry on with life as usual? Someone has to stick around and deal with what lurks in the dark corners of the room. In other words, solutions come from proximity." **Danielle Strickland, *Better Together*, Chapter 6**

 READ

For by the grace given me I say to every one of you: Do not think of yourself more highly than you ought, but rather think of yourself with sober judgment, in accordance with the faith God has distributed to each of you. For just as each of us has one body with many members, and these members do not all have the same function, so in Christ we, though many, form one body, and each member belongs to all the others. (**Romans 12:3–5**)

 CONSIDER

How might I think of myself more highly than I ought to? Make an honest assessment and list the areas or ways here.

How can I see myself and others in Christ as valued members of the same body? Describe what this would look like in your daily life as well as in a forward, future-thinking way of life.

_____

_____

_____

_____

 STEP OUT

Review your group goals from Day 2 of last session's Personal Study (pages 48–49). Consider how you are moving forward with each goal and how you are not? Note any areas of anxiety or shame, and invite God into those places. Think through some practical ways that you can continue to take steps forward.

 PRAY

Ask God to help you think through ways you are valuable to the body of Christ. Spend time listening to what he has to say. Consider inviting a friend into this prayer process with you so that God can help you both uplift one another.

_____

_____

_____

_____

_____

LOOKING FOR MORE?

Read Chapter 7 of _Better Together_ by Danielle Strickland and write down what stands out to you most.

DAY · 2

"The community began to see the church leading from relationship and unity, a shared leadership model—no longer competing with each other but collaborating for others." **Danielle Strickland,** *Better Together,* **Chapter 5**

 READ

There are different kinds of gifts, but the same Spirit distributes them. There are different kinds of service, but the same Lord. There are different kinds of working, but in all of them and in everyone it is the same God at work. **(1 Corinthians 12:4–6)**

 CONSIDER

How have I seen God empower women in Christ with his Holy Spirit? List those instances here. Make note of the result of these examples of empowerment.

_____

_____

_____

_____

_____

What are the different opportunities I have to empower the women around me? List them here.

_____

_____

_____

_____

 **STEP OUT**

Organize a group of both women and men to work together on something positive in your community. It can be a canned food drive, a forum to discuss diversity, a way to support single parents, etc. The point is to plan and execute it as a team. Notice how the group's differences helped, or how they created tension. Debrief the experience together when you are done.

 PRAY

Ask God how he wants to empower you today and spend some time opening up your heart to that empowerment. Ask him how he might use you to empower the women around you.

_____

_____

_____

_____

_____

_____

_____

_____

_____

_____

LOOKING FOR MORE?

Read all of 1 Corinthians 12. How are we as the body of Christ better together?

DAY · 3

"Without proximity there is no impact. You can hold all the opinions you want on gender equality but if you don't have an integrated leadership team you will not be part of transforming the future."
Danielle Strickland, *Better Together*, Chapter 6

 READ

Make every effort to keep the unity of the Spirit through the bond of peace. There is one body and one Spirit, just as you were called to one hope when you were called; one Lord, one faith, one baptism; one God and Father of all, who is over all and through all and in all. **(Ephesians 4:3–6)**

 CONSIDER

What could oneness look like in the body of Christ? How can I play my part in *keeping the unity of the Spirit through the bond of peace*?

_____

_____

_____

_____

_____

_____

_____

 STEP OUT

Text someone with a completely different gifting and/or perspective and affirm them for the way you see God moving in or through them.

PRAY

Knowing you are fully forgiven and accepted in Christ, talk to God about areas where it is difficult for you to embrace difference in this world. Ask him to reveal any areas of fear that have led or may lead to prejudice.

_____

_____

_____

_____

_____

_____

_____

_____

_____

_____

_____

_____

_____

_____

_____

_____

_____

◌◌ LOOKING FOR MORE?

Read Chapter 8 of _Better Together_ by Danielle Strickland and write down what stands out to you most.

Notes

Replacing Root Beliefs

Group Gathering

WARM UP (5–10 minutes)

INVITE GOD IN

Take a few minutes to talk with God silently about what you are bringing with you into this Group Gathering. What might distract you? What might be good to share with the group? Sit with God and take an inventory of what is on your heart right now.

If it is helpful, use the space below to write, draw, or express yourself to God.

_____

_____

_____

_____

_____

_____

_____

DISCUSS TOGETHER

What does it mean to truly believe something? How do your beliefs impact the way you live and act? What decisions and postures, reactions and responses are directly influenced by your beliefs versus cultural or peer influence?

WATCH VIDEO (21 minutes)

Watch the video for Group Gathering 5. Feel free to take notes in the space provided.

VIDEO NOTES

_____

_____

_____

_____

Nothing will change without changing ourselves.

"We will not change any system or structure or culture or our world without changing ourselves."

_____

_____

_____

_____

Identify some key beliefs.

"Take some time to identify key beliefs that are contributing to your values and actions and producing the wrong kinds of fruit in your relationships and leaderships."

_____

_____

_____

_____

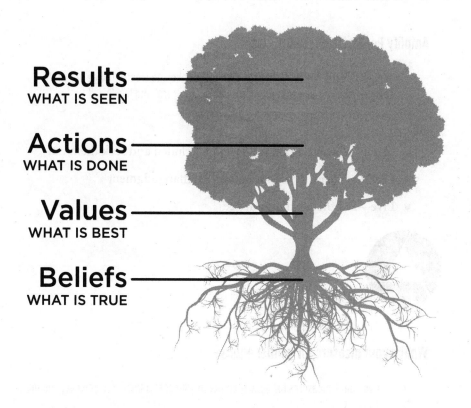

Results
WHAT IS SEEN

Actions
WHAT IS DONE

Values
WHAT IS BEST

Beliefs
WHAT IS TRUE

Trace fruit to actions, actions to values, and values to root beliefs.

"What if we trace the fruit in our lives to our actions and our actions to our values and our values to our rooted beliefs?"

_____

_____

_____

_____

_____

_____

Amplify Peace: Listen, Learn, Live

> "Amplify peace, a movement of global peacemakers to create change in people and communities and cultures. It's called listen, learn, and live."

- **Listen**—Pay attention to WHO is excluded and seek them out
- **Learn**—Curiosity is more powerful than judgment
- **Live**—Put theory into practice

_____

_____

_____

_____

What's your measure for gender equity?

> "Do you have measures for gender equity in your community? Are you even aiming for it?"

_____

_____

_____

TAKE A MOMENT

Take two minutes to jot down what stood out to you the most about what Danielle said. What resonated with you, and what was challenging?

_____

_____

_____

_____

UNPACK TOGETHER (35–45 minutes)

DISCUSS TOGETHER

1. Danielle said that actions can be traced to values and values to root beliefs. What kind of values might cause someone to approach gender equality/equity in a misinformed way? What might be the root beliefs behind those values?

2. How can the process of *listen, learn, and live* be helpful in changing our root beliefs? What makes differing perspectives and experiences so important to shifting these beliefs?

Those Who Did Not Desert Jesus:

Select a volunteer to read aloud to the group:

When the soldiers crucified Jesus, they took his clothes, dividing them into four shares, one for each of them, with the undergarment remaining. This garment was seamless, woven in one piece from top to bottom. "Let's not tear it," they said to one another. "Let's decide by lot who will get it." This happened that the scripture might be fulfilled that said, "They divided my clothes among them and cast lots for my garment." So this is what the soldiers did. Near the cross of Jesus stood his mother, his mother's sister, Mary the wife of Clopas, and Mary Magdalene. **(John 19:23–25)**

EXPLORE TOGETHER

Group leader, read the following passage and commentary aloud. Discuss the questions below.

No good tree bears bad fruit, nor does a bad tree bear good fruit. Each tree is recognized by its own fruit. People do not pick figs from

77

thornbushes, or grapes from briers. A good man brings good things out of the good stored up in his heart, and an evil man brings evil things out of the evil stored up in his heart. For the mouth speaks what the heart is full of. **(Luke 6:43–45)**

What It Meant Then:

Jesus is midway through his Sermon on the Plain, a discourse in which he challenges the root beliefs of his time around love, judgment, and blessing. A diverse crowd had gathered around Jesus made up of his disciples, Jews from around Judah, and those coming from nearby Gentile regions. Jesus flips conventional belief on its head, pronouncing blessing for the poor, hungry, weeping, and persecuted. The centerpiece of the new upside-down kingdom that he is ushering in is found in his radical and unheard-of call to "love your enemies" and "do good to those who hate you" (Luke 6:27). This is the context on which verses 43–45 are built.

In the passage, Jesus reveals a powerful truth about the human heart: our words and actions flow from the depths of our inner self. Using the example of a tree and its fruit, he points out that the fruit in someone's life (their words and actions) are a direct result of the tree they are growing from (a person's heart). No lasting change in the fruit is possible without transformation to the tree itself.

What It Means Now:

Jesus was pointing out something that neurologists and psychologists have only recently started to unpack. We are finding more and more evidence that action and decision making grow out of deep-seated beliefs in the inner self. Though they are not always easily identified, the impact of painful memories, the repeated embrace of lies, and falsely held beliefs all shape how we interact with the world around us, others, and even God. For sustainable change to occur, an inside-out approach is necessary.

But how do we impact the heart in this way so that we can bring about change in our actions and words? Jesus seems to offer some clues in the verses immediately following 43–45. He says that "everyone who comes to me and hears my words and puts them into practice" is like one who builds a house on rock, a stable and trustworthy foundation.

Coming to Jesus is the first step in changing root beliefs. This is not something that we can do without his transformative power. Next Jesus identifies the importance of *hearing his words*. This is where Jesus wants to replace our misguided beliefs with the truth. These truths can come from Scripture, a trusted friend, or the Holy Spirit himself. And finally—and perhaps most importantly—he points out the need for us to put our new beliefs *into practice*. As we repeatedly live from and allow our actions to flow from these new beliefs, they will become more and more ingrained into our inner self.

1. How would Jesus' claim that bad fruit comes from a bad tree be challenging to those who were listening? In what way is this truth connected to Jesus' teaching on radical love for others?

2. Where have you seen someone's inner beliefs impact the way they live and act? How are root beliefs impacting gender inequality in our world?

3. What core beliefs (both negative and positive) might be impacting your approach to the shared thriving of women and men? Which of those beliefs might Jesus want to transform in you so that the fruit that grows from your heart can be changed?

EXPERIENCE TOGETHER

Supplies:

- Pens

- Scissors

Instructions:

- Have each member of the group take a few minutes to themselves to prayerfully fill in the Fruit, Actions, and Values sections of the worksheet on the next page. Members will be identifying a false belief and corresponding actions that they want Jesus to challenge and ultimately transform.

- Split into groups of two or three and share the fruit you don't like, the actions, and the values you wrote down.

- Use the bottom of the worksheet as you take turns together in your smaller group to prayerfully identify one or more truths that God wants to give each person as a replacement for that false root belief.

- Have each person fill in the blank line at the bottom of the worksheet and say the prayer on page 84 aloud with the smaller group. Then have the other member or two of the smaller group pray over the person who has shared.

- Once everyone is done, cut out the prayer on page 84 and put it in a place that will remind all of you to continue praying and putting into practice the truth God has given you.

These truths may take time, practice, and continued prayer to be fully embraced. It is helpful to make a habit of continuing this prayer process of rejecting false beliefs and embracing truth in Jesus' name both in your personal time and in community.

PRAY TOGETHER

Have someone close your time in prayer by inviting God into the rest of this week.

Name the fruit in your life you don't like.

ACTIONS
Name your actions related to the bad fruit.

- _____
- _____
- _____

VALUES
Name the values informing your actions.

- _____
- _____
- _____
- _____

ROOT BELIEF(S)
Name the root belief that needs to change.

_____

CONFESSING FALSE BELIEF

Ask God to help you identify a root belief in your heart (in full or in part) that is causing unwanted fruit in your life around the area of gender equality. If needed, use the list of false beliefs below. Once you have identified the root belief, write down a few areas where you see that belief impacting your words, thoughts, or actions.

God, I confess that I, in whole or in part, falsely believe _____ _____ . Thank you for your grace and forgiveness in Jesus Christ. I also confess that that belief has led me to think, speak, and act in the following ways:

_____

_____

_____

_____

False Beliefs

- Women/Men are less valuable.

- Women/Men are less intelligent.

- Women/Men are less capable.

- Women/Men cannot be trusted.

- Women/Men are inherently promiscuous.

- Women/Men are inherently evil.

- Women/Men are more sinful.

- Women/Men can be used as objects.

- Women/Men exist for my pleasure.

- Lust for a woman/man doesn't hurt anybody.

- I, as a woman/man, am unlovable.

- I cannot be led by a woman/man.

- God loves me less if I am a woman/man.

- God cares for me less if I am a woman/man.

- God cannot work through me if I am a woman/man.

- God cannot work through a woman/man as powerfully.

CLAIMING TRUTH IN CHRIST

With one or two other people in your group, share the belief and actions you wrote down above. In this smaller group, take turns prayerfully identifying one or more truths that God wants to give each person as a replacement for that root belief. If needed, use the list of truths below but do not let it limit you. God may reveal to your group a truth that is special for you.

I reject the false belief _____ as a lie in Jesus' name. God, I instead embrace your truth _____.
Thank you, Lord, for starting this transforming work in my heart.

Replacement Truths

- Both male and female are made in God's image (Genesis 1:27).

- God can work powerfully through both women and men (Luke 1:30–31; 2:36–38; John 20:18; Acts 18:26; etc.).

- God created me/others with good works prepared for me/them to do (Ephesians 2:10).

- God loves and values me/others immensely regardless of gender (John 3:16).

- I am called to value others above myself regardless of gender (Philippians 2:3–4).

- In Christ, I am / others are children of God (Galatians 3:26).

- I am / Others are fully forgiven in Christ (Colossians 3:13).

- All have fallen short, but all are freely justified in Christ (Romans 3:23–24).

Personal Study

The following pages are for your personal study in between sessions. Engage in any or all of these three times of prayer and reflection in order to enhance your experience.

DAY · 1

"Shifting a mindset is a deeply difficult process, but it also holds the most transformational opportunity for change. Without a mindset shift you may change structures, systems, and institutions, but those changes rarely last. What we believe is at the root of everything we do." **Danielle Strickland, *Better Together*, Chapter 8**

 READ

Blind Pharisee! First clean the inside of the cup and dish, and then the outside also will be clean. **(Matthew 23:26)**

 CONSIDER

In what ways do I try to clean up my outside perception without inviting Jesus to transform my heart? Note and describe the positive and negative consequences here.

_____

_____

_____

_____

_____

_____

 **STEP OUT**

Have a conversation with someone of the opposite gender about one truth you are learning from Jesus right now concerning gender equality.

 PRAY

Ask God to reveal what area of your heart he wants you to open to his transformation. Offer that part of your heart to him and ask for his healing.

_____

_____

_____

_____

_____

_____

_____

_____

_____

_____

_____

_____

_____

LOOKING FOR MORE?

Read Chapter 9 of *Better Together* by Danielle Strickland and write down what stands out to you most.

DAY · 2

"If you don't like the results of your life you cannot just pick off the fruit and call it a day. You must look at your actions, which will reveal your values and expose your false beliefs. To change the quality of our life's output will require us to replant true beliefs that will grow better fruit." **Danielle Strickland, *Better Together*, Chapter 8**

 READ

Remain in me, as I also remain in you. No branch can bear fruit by itself; it must remain in the vine. Neither can you bear fruit unless you remain in me. I am the vine; you are the branches. If you remain in me and I in you, you will bear much fruit; apart from me you can do nothing. **(John 15:4–5)**

The word "remain" can also be translated "abide." In other words, make your home in Jesus.

 CONSIDER

How do I try to live, grow, and change myself apart from God? What would it look like to make my home with Jesus so that he can bring about fruit in and through my life? What would this shift actually and practically look like? What aspects of my life would be affected?

 **STEP OUT**

Spend some time with God unearthing some more false beliefs that he wants to replace with truth. Use the prayer below as a template from which to start your prayer.

I reject the false belief _____ as a lie in Jesus' name.
God, I instead embrace your truth _____. Thank you,
Lord, for starting this transforming work in my heart.

 PRAY

Spend at least five minutes just resting in Jesus' presence. Practice abiding in him.

_____

_____

_____

_____

_____

_____

_____

_____

_____

_____

 LOOKING FOR MORE?

Read all of John 15. What do you learn about relying on Christ in growth and transformation?

DAY · 3

"We convince ourselves that doing nothing will buy us time and stall the inevitable changes that are necessary. But it doesn't. *Doing nothing is an action.* It cements the ways of the status quo and creates a paralysis that prevents any change from emerging." **Danielle Strickland,** *Better Together,* **Chapter 5**

 READ

Very truly I [Jesus] tell you, whoever believes in me will do the works I have been doing, and they will do even greater things than these, because I am going to the Father. And I will do whatever you ask in my name, so that the Father may be glorified in the Son. You may ask me for anything in my name, and I will do it. **(John 14:12–14)**

 CONSIDER

How does Jesus want these words to apply to me? How can I impact gender equality for the good in his name? Describe your responses here.

_____

_____

_____

_____

_____

_____

 STEP OUT

Post to your social media or text a friend a verse from the Bible or a quote from *Better Together* that promotes the truth about gender equality/equity.

PRAY

Ask Jesus what he wants you to ask for in his name that would help you to do even greater things than he has done. Spend some time listening and then ask for what he reveals to you.

_____

_____

_____

_____

_____

_____

_____

_____

_____

_____

_____

_____

_____

_____

_____

_____

_____

LOOKING FOR MORE?

Read Chapter 10 of _Better Together_ by Danielle Strickland and write down what stands out to you most.

Notes

Session 6:
Transition to Thriving

Group Gathering

WARM UP (5–10 minutes)

INVITE GOD IN

Take a few minutes to recount with God your experience in this study. What is your greatest takeaway as you step into this last Group Gathering? How do you want to be different as you step into the future?

If it is helpful, use the space below to write, draw, or express yourself to God.

_____

_____

_____

_____

_____

DISCUSS TOGETHER

What is the most difficult part of transition? How is transitioning into a way of life especially difficult? What do you think is the greatest cause for resisting transition? Is it rational or irrational?

WATCH VIDEO (22 minutes)

Watch the video for Group Gathering 6. Feel free to take notes in the space provided.

VIDEO NOTES

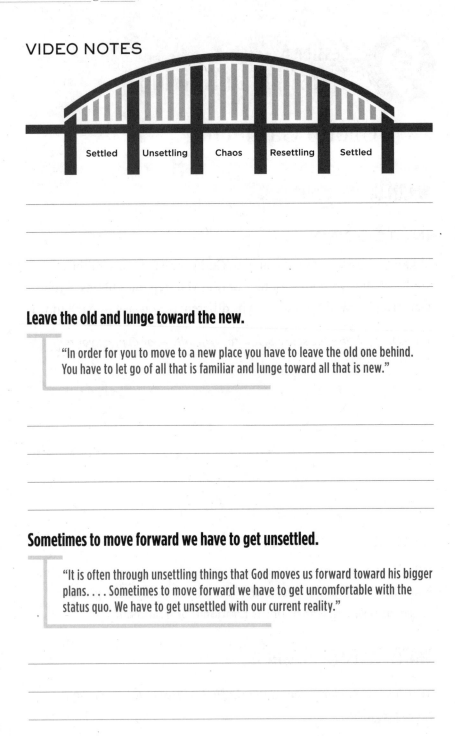

Settled   Unsettling   Chaos   Resettling   Settled

Leave the old and lunge toward the new.

> "In order for you to move to a new place you have to leave the old one behind. You have to let go of all that is familiar and lunge toward all that is new."

Sometimes to move forward we have to get unsettled.

> "It is often through unsettling things that God moves us forward toward his bigger plans. . . . Sometimes to move forward we have to get uncomfortable with the status quo. We have to get unsettled with our current reality."

Acts 10 – Peter's Vision

_____

_____

_____

_____

_____

Women and men need to cross the bridge together.

> "God knew that for transition to occur, for the division to be healed, for enemies to become friends, they would need to cross the bridge together. Nowhere is this more true than for women and men."

_____

_____

_____

_____

_____

Leaving behind what we know is an act of faith.

> "Leaving behind what we know for what God wants to show us is an act of faith. It will require us to trust God more, to depend on God more, to lean on each other, to need each other in new ways."

_____

_____

_____

_____

95

Hope is alive and active.

> "Hope is alive and active and ready to infuse us to dream and live out those dreams in our time."

_____

_____

_____

_____

_____

Ephesians 3:14–21 – Paul's Prayer

_____

_____

_____

_____

TAKE A MOMENT

Take two minutes to jot down what stood out to you the most about what Danielle said. What resonated with you, and what was challenging?

_____

_____

_____

_____

_____

UNPACK TOGETHER (35–45 minutes)

DISCUSS TOGETHER

1. Considering the transition bridge Danielle laid out (Settled, Unsettled, Chaos, Resettling, Settled), what do you think is most unsettling about change (especially considering gender equity)? How can a willingness to *disturb the present* help to create the shared thriving of women and men in the future?

2. How can men support women in the Chaos stage of our transition to a better future? How can women support men?

Settling into A New Reality:

Select a volunteer to read aloud to the group:

Now Mary stood outside the tomb crying. As she wept, she bent over to look into the tomb and saw two angels in white, seated where Jesus' body had been, one at the head and the other at the foot. They asked her, "Woman, why are you crying?" "They have taken my Lord away," she said, "and I don't know where they have put him." At this, she turned around and saw Jesus standing there, but she did not realize that it was Jesus. He asked her, "Woman, why are you crying? Who is it you are looking for?" Thinking he was the gardener, she said, "Sir, if you have carried him away, tell me where you have put him, and I will get him." Jesus said to her, "Mary." She turned toward him and cried out in Aramaic, "Rabboni!" (which means "Teacher"). **(John 20:11–16)**

EXPLORE TOGETHER

Group leader, read the following passage and commentary aloud.
Discuss the questions below.

This is what the LORD says—he who made a way through the sea,
a path through the mighty waters, who drew out the chariots and
horses, the army and reinforcements together, and they lay there, never
to rise again, extinguished, snuffed out like a wick: "Forget the former
things; do not dwell on the past. See, I am doing a new thing! Now it
springs up; do you not perceive it? I am making a way in the wilderness
and streams in the wasteland." **(Isaiah 43:16–19)**

What It Meant Then:

The book of Isaiah offers a message of both judgment and hope to the
people of Israel. Isaiah's prophecy rightly predicts the Babylonian exile
more than a hundred years before its occurrence and calls on Israel to
repent of their wickedness. Instead Israel's hearts are hardened, leading
them ultimately toward their own ruin. The book of Isaiah time and
time again sets up the hopelessness of Israel's situation.

But through Isaiah, God reveals that even in this most impossible
of circumstances, he still will bring deliverance. The extravagantly
opposed language of the verses above demonstrates this fact. A "way"
is not something easily found in the wilderness and a "steam" flowing
in a wasteland is unheard of. God uses this imagery to describe the
miraculous nature of the "new thing" he is about to do. He even
compares it to the Israelites' exodus from Egypt in verse 16, saying that
this is something to forget in comparison to what he has coming. This
would have been a radical statement considering the importance of
that story in Israelite culture.

Though undoubtedly pointing forward to Israel's return from exile,
in Isaiah God unearths a much larger salvation work that is to come.

The prophet reveals that God's judgment is for the sake of cleansing his people and that he will grow a shoot of new life from the stump that Israel has become (Isaiah 11:1). This new shoot will come in the form of a suffering Servant King who will be the Messiah of all humanity.

His unending rule will bring transformation to all nations, redeem humankind, and end suffering and death forever (Isaiah 24–27). He will be called Immanuel, meaning "God with us," and will bring good news to the poor, brokenhearted, and captives (Isaiah 7:14; 61:1).

Hundreds of years later, Jesus identifies himself as this Messianic King described in Isaiah (see Luke 4:18; 9:18–27), going on to suffer and die for the sake of all humanity. But after three days God raises him to new life, conquering sin

> The word "poor" in Isaiah 61 encompasses not only the impoverished but also others on the fringes of society. This would have included: women, children, elderly, sick, social outsiders, sinners, those of other nationalities and races.

and death forever. The new thing God reveals in the Isaiah 61 passage is that in Jesus he will create a way for all nations to be delivered from the otherwise hopeless wasteland of sin and death.

What It Means Now:

As we approach the end of this study, it is helpful for us to consider the transition we are making. In forgetting the former things in favor of embracing the new thing God is doing, Jesus is inviting us to follow him into a new order of things. This new reality is one where all humanity is seen through God's eyes and we uplift those who have been stamped down. As we continue to cross this transition bridge, there will surely be discomfort and chaos. The good news is we do not have to trust in our own strength to get across. We have Christ, our stream in a desolate wasteland, and he has given us each other. We can march toward our future, better together.

1. How was God's incredible promise from Isaiah important for Israel in the face of hopelessness? What difficulty might they have in forgetting the former things despite the good new thing God was doing?

2. How can the promise of Jesus' new reality still bring someone hope today? Where do you see people having difficulty transitioning to that reality?

3. How does God's ability to make a way in the wilderness bring you hope for the shared thriving of women and men? What areas do you imagine feeling unsettled and chaotic as you make that transition?

EXPERIENCE TOGETHER

Supplies:

- Four chairs

- Basketball or volleyball

Instructions:

- Make a transition bridge of your own using chairs and a basketball or volleyball (with the ball in the middle and two chairs on either side). The four chairs and the ball represent the five stages of the transition bridge (Settled, Unsettled, Chaos, Resettling, Settled).

- Select a specific area of inequality or disunity among women and men in your community, church, or group that would benefit by transitioning toward the shared thriving of women and men. (Be sure to select something you can continue to impact as a group as you move forward from this study guide. You can even use one of your group goals from Session 3 (pages 48–49).

- Have one person from your group step up onto the first chair and begin to cross the transition bridge. At each stage have them stop as you discuss your group's selected area of transition and what makes it so difficult to move from one stage of transition to the next. Have them stay at one stage until you have come up with ways that you as a group can continue to support one another and find the support of Christ in that particular stage.

- Make sure you have a couple of people spotting the person on the bridge and helping them to cross the Chaos stage safely.

PRAY TOGETHER

Take a little extra time in this last Group Gathering to ask Jesus to bring his kingdom on earth as it is in heaven. Each of you listen for the areas that he might want you to pray for. Think of one area of inequality or oppression you want eliminated and one area of hope or unity you want emphasized. Take turns saying aloud, "God, instead of _____, bring _____ today." Leave enough space for everyone to pray aloud at least once. Have someone close in prayer by asking God to help your group to continue praying for and working toward the shared thriving of both women and men.

Personal Study

The following pages are for your personal study in between sessions. Engage in any or all of these three times of prayer and reflection in order to enhance your experience.

DAY · 1

> "It feels like chaos. Everyone has these moments. We leave the old behind and launch into the new—even before we are steady or feel ready. We could even call this the 'faith' zone—where we are required to leap before we fully understand." **Danielle Strickland, *Better Together*, Chapter 13**

 READ

Forget the former things; do not dwell on the past. See, I am doing a new thing! Now it springs up; do you not perceive it? I am making a way in the wilderness and streams in the wasteland. **(Isaiah 43:18–19)**

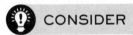 **CONSIDER**

What parts of the culture around me might I need to let go of in order to embrace the new culture Jesus has established? What would it look like to start letting go of those parts of the old culture? Make a plan. Write it down. Claim action over passive compassion.

_____

_____

_____

_____

 **STEP OUT**

Choose one day this week to completely fast from screens (TV, phone games, social media, web browsing, etc.). Spend the time you would on a screen instead in prayer for the community and culture around you and in fellowship with both women and men.

 PRAY

Talk to God about the *wilderness* and *wastelands* you see around you (areas that do not seem like they could ever change). Ask him to show you how he is making *a way in that wilderness and streams in those wastelands*. Ask him how you can play a part in that *new thing* that he is doing.

_____

_____

_____

_____

_____

_____

_____

_____

_____

_____

LOOKING FOR MORE?

Read Chapter 11 of *Better Together* by Danielle Strickland and write down what stands out to you most.

DAY · 2

"One of the most powerful and obvious parts of the experience is that no one can transition alone without crashing and burning in the middle. Talk to each other. Take care of each other. Ask for help as you navigate your way." **Danielle Strickland, *Better Together*, Chapter 13**

 READ

The Lord is near. Do not be anxious about anything, but in every situation, by prayer and petition, with thanksgiving, present your requests to God. And the peace of God, which transcends all understanding, will guard your hearts and your minds in Christ Jesus. **(Philippians 4:5b–7)**

 CONSIDER

Where am I feeling anxious about moving from an area of settledness into an area of chaos as I transition into Jesus' new culture? Who can I ask to support me in that shift?

_____

_____

_____

_____

What are some tools I am going to need or that I can take advantage of in order to move from one area to another and to literally shift my perspective and posture?

_____

_____

_____

_____

 **STEP OUT**

Ask one or two trusted friends if you can all support and encourage one another as you seek to embrace the new culture Jesus is setting up. Create a regular opportunity for you all to check in on one another and pray for each other.

 PRAY

Give God thanks for the peace that he has offered you in the past and spend time inviting his peace into areas of anxiety for you.

_____

_____

_____

_____

_____

_____

_____

_____

_____

_____

LOOKING FOR MORE?

Read all of Philippians 4. What do you learn about peace from this chapter? How can that be helpful to us in the unsettledness or chaos of transition to the mutual thriving of both women and men?

DAY · 3

"God invited humanity to co-create together. Resisting 'men' fixing the problem or 'women' dominating the discussion, the invitation in this stretch is to navigate the way together, just like we were created to do." **Danielle Strickland, *Better Together*, Chapter 1**

 READ

The LORD himself goes before you and will be with you; he will never leave you nor forsake you. Do not be afraid; do not be discouraged. **(Deuteronomy 31:8)**

 CONSIDER

When considering moving toward the shared thriving of men and women, what would it look like to move forward with that transition knowing that *the Lord himself goes before me and will be with me?*

_____

_____

_____

_____

Define what thriving means to you now. Define the who, what, where, how, and the impact into the future.

_____

_____

_____

_____

Write a personal declaration of commitment to being an agent of change toward living in a world where women and men *are* better together. Claim your your part in transitioning to thriving. Share your declaration with others in a few different contexts where you can be held accountable in love and kindness.

_____

_____

_____

_____

STEP OUT

Do something intentional today to promote the shared thriving of women and men. It can be releasing control of a project, posting to your social media, or elevating the voice of a woman. Get creative and courageous! Know that God *will never leave you nor forsake you.*

PRAY

Pray through a time in your life when you felt alone or left by God. Ask God if he would show you where he was at that time and how he was with you. Ask him what healing might look like in that place.

_____

_____

_____

_____

_____

LOOKING FOR MORE?

Read Chapter 12 of *Better Together* by Danielle Strickland and write down what stands out to you most.

Notes

References

Biblica, the International Bible Society. "Intro to Jeremiah." Introduction from the NIV Study Bible, used with permission from Zondervan. Biblica .com. https://www.biblica.com/resources/scholar-notes/niv-study-bible/intro -to-jeremiah/ (accessed August 2, 2019).

The Bible Project. "1 Corinthians." TheBibleProject.com. https://thebible project.com/explore/1-corinthians/ (accessed September 25, 2019).

The Bible Project. "Galatians." TheBibleProject.com. https://thebibleproject .com/explore/galatians/ (accessed September 17, 2019).

The Bible Project. "Isaiah." TheBibleProject.com. https://thebibleproject.com /explore/isaiah/ (accessed September 27, 2019).

The Bible Project. "Jeremiah." TheBibleProject.com. https://thebibleproject .com/explore/jeremiah/ (accessed August 2, 2019).

The Bible Project. "John." TheBibleProject.com. https://thebibleproject.com /explore/john/ (accessed September 11, 2019).

The Bible Project. "Luke." TheBibleProject.com. https://thebibleproject.com /explore/luke/ (accessed September 27, 2019).

The Bible Project. "Luke–Acts Miniseries." TheBibleProject.com. https://the bibleproject.com/explore/gospel-series/ (accessed September 27, 2019).

Bock, Darrell L. *Luke*. Baker Exegetical Commentary on the New Testament, edited by Moisés Silva. Grand Rapids, MI: Baker Academic, 1994.

de Boer, Martinus C. *Galatians, A Commentary*. The New Testament Library. Louisville, KY: Westminster John Knox Press, 2011.

Kistemaker, Simon J. *Exposition of the First Epistle to the Corinthians*. The New Testament Library. Grand Rapids, MI: Baker Academic, 1993.

Moo, Douglas J. *Galatians*. Baker Exegetical Commentary on the New Testament, edited by Robert W. Yarbrough and Robert H. Stein. Grand Rapids, MI: Baker Academic, 2013.

Oswalt, John N. *The Book of Isaiah: Chapters 1–39*. Volume of The New International Commentary on the Old Testament, edited by R.K. Harrison and Robert L. Hubbard Jr. Grand Rapids, MI: Wm. B. Eerdmans Publishing Co., 1986.

Strickland, Danielle. *Better Together*. Nashville, TN: Thomas Nelson, 2020.

Thompson, J. A. *Jeremiah*. The New International Commentary on the Old Testament, edited by R. K. Harrison and Robert L. Hubbard Jr. Grand Rapids, MI: Wm. B. Eerdmans Publishing Co., 1980.

Thompson, Marianne Meye. *John, A Commentary*. The New Testament Library. Louisville, KY: Westminster John Knox Press, 2015.

Whitacre, Rodney A. *John*. The IVP New Testament Commentary Series, edited by Grant R. Osborne. Downers Grove, IL: IVP Academic, 1999.

Williams, Sam K. *Galatians*. Abingdon New Testament Commentaries. Nashville, TN: Abingdon Press, 1997.

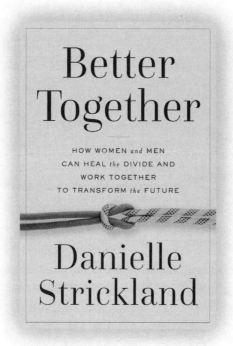